THE GOSPEL OF JESUS CHRIST
A KINGDOM CONCEPT

BY PIERCE A. SMITH

Copyright © 2019 by Pierce A. Smith

All rights reserved. No part of this publication may be reproduced by any means, graphics, electronic, or mechanical, including photocopying, recording, taping, or by any information storage retrieval system without the written permission of the publisher except in the case of brief quotations embodied in critical articles and reviews.

Pierce A. Smith/Rejoice Essential Publishing
PO BOX 512
Effingham, SC 29541

www.republishing.org

Unless otherwise indicated, scripture is taken from the New King James Version.

Scripture quotations marked (NKJV) are taken from the New King James Version®. Copyright © 1982 by Thomas Nelson. Used by permission. All rights reserved.

Scripture quotations marked (NLT) are taken from the Holy Bible, New Living Translation, copyright ©1996, 2004, 2015 by Tyndale House Foundation. Used by permission of Tyndale House Publishers, Inc., Carol Stream, Illinois 60188. All rights reserved.

Scripture quotations marked AMPC are taken from the Amplified® Bible (AMPC), Copyright © 1954, 1958, 1962, 1964, 1965, 1987 by The Lockman Foundation Used by permission. www.Lockman.org"

Scripture quotations marked (NIV) are taken from the Holy Bible, New International Version®, NIV®. Copyright © 1973, 1978, 1984, 2011 by Biblica, Inc.™ Used by permission of Zondervan. All rights reserved worldwide. www.zondervan.com The "NIV" and "New International Version" are trademarks registered in the United States Patent and Trademark Office by Biblica, Inc.™

Quotations designated (NET) are from the NET Bible® copyright ©1996-2018 by Biblical Studies Press, L.L.C. http://netbible.com All rights reserved.

Author's website: www.abundantglory.org

The Gospel of Jesus Christ/ Pierce A. Smith

ISBN-10: 1-946756-72-5

ISBN-13: 978-1-946756-72-5

Library of Congress Number: 2019914353

TABLE OF CONTENTS

PREFACE..ix

CHAPTER 1: God Has a Government..........................1

CHAPTER 2: Why Knowing About God's Government is Important........................13

CHAPTER 3: What Is the Gospel of the Kingdom..................27

CHAPTER 4: Is the Gospel of the Kingdom Relevant Today..................46

CHAPTER 5: Fulfilling One's Destiny..............................55

CHAPTER 6: Final Thoughts on the Kingdom of God................................64

ABOUT THE AUTHOR..76

DEDICATION

I dedicate this book to my lovely wife, Thelma, whose encouragement and guidance made it possible for me to do this book. Also, I would like to dedicate this book to my parents, Jeanette Smith and Rev. W. Pierce Smith, whose wisdom, prayer life and guidance, helped me to get where I am. Last but not least, I thank God for my children Cheri, Dawn and Pierce II who also have been an inspiration and blessing to Thelma and I.

PREFACE

Years ago, though I believed in Jesus Christ as my Lord and Savior, I didn't understand Scriptures like Matthew 6:33 "But seek first the Kingdom of God and His righteousness, and all these things shall be added to you." I believe the reason I did not understand this was because Jesus was telling me to seek the Kingdom of God first when I was always taught to seek Jesus first. So, naturally, with my inquisitive mind, I wanted to know why Jesus was telling me to seek His Kingdom first and not Him? Then in Matthew 4:23, it said, "And Jesus went about all Galilee, teaching in their synagogues, **preaching the gospel of the Kingdom**, and healing all kinds of sickness and all kinds of disease among the people." So, I began to wonder, "Why would Jesus preach the gospel of the Kingdom if it wasn't important?"

Then one day, I heard the late Dr. Myles Munroe teach on the Kingdom of God. In fact, I downloaded two of his books to my iPad. One was called *"Rediscovering the Kingdom"*[1] and the second was *"Kingdom Principles: Preparing for Kingdom Experience and Expansion."*[2] I became so hungry for understanding God's Kingdom that I did a study on my own, listening to anyone I could find about the Kingdom of God. The more I studied the subject; the clearer things began to appear to me, little by little, as it related to salvation and the subject of God's wonderful grace towards mankind. This book is a small compilation of some things that I have found.

Jesus challenged the norm of His days, and ultimately, was crucified for it. Yet, what Jesus was preaching, and teaching was what God, the Father, was saying and doing. The religious leaders of Jesus' days did not fully understand the Old Testament writings either and, therefore, tried to stick with the old way of looking at things. They did not understand that the Old Testament was actually pointing to Jesus Christ. They did not understand that what they were taught was simply to hold them until Christ comes. They did not understand the mystery that the apostle Paul stated in Romans.

Romans 3:19, 20 (NLT), "Obviously, the law applies to those to whom it was given, for its purpose is to keep people from having excuses, and to show that the entire world is guilty before God. 20 For no one can ever be made right with God by doing what the law commands. The law simply shows us how sinful we are."

The religious leaders of Jesus' days did not understand Galatians 3:10, 11 (NLT) which says, "But those who depend on the law to make them right with God are under His curse, for the Scriptures say, "Cursed is everyone who does not observe and obey all the commands that are written in God's Book of the Law." 11 So it is clear that no one can be made right with God by trying to keep the law. For the Scriptures say, "It is through faith that a righteous person has life."

The religious leaders of Jesus' days did not understand Galatians 3:19 (NLT) where it says, "Why, then, was the law given? It was given alongside the promise to show people their sins. But the law was designed to last only until the coming of the child who was promised. God gave His law through angels

---

1 Rediscovering the Kingdom Expanded Edition—Ancient Hope For Our 21st Century World, Copyright 2010, Destiny Image Publishers, Inc. Shippensburg, PA 17257

to Moses, who was the mediator between God and the people."

Galatians 3:21 (NLT) "Is there a conflict, then, between God's law and God's promises? Absolutely not! If the law could give us new life, we could be made right with God by obeying it."

Since what the religious leaders were teaching in Jesus' days was the norm, they could not see that God was disgusted with their hypocrisy and that the way of faith was always God's original plan.

So, what is the purpose of this book? I will try to inspire Christians to have a better understanding and appreciation of what Jesus came to give to the world. I will try to help them know some of the why's of their salvation, its importance, and why I believe we, as a Church, overall, have gotten away from the Kingdom message. Lastly, hopefully, we all can have a better understanding of the 'why' of our personal journeys with the Lord. In other words, the purpose of this book is to teach others about the Kingdom of God.

---

2 Understanding the Kingdom—Preparing for Kingdom Experience and Expansion, Copyright 2006, Destiny Image Publishers, Inc. Shippensburg, PA 17257

I hope this book creates a hunger and thirst in you so that you too will want to know more about God's Kingdom. I pray that you enjoy it as you read it and that it would answer a lot of your questions about the Gospel of Jesus Christ.

CHAPTER 1

GOD HAS A GOVERNMENT

Where did the idea of God having a government begin in the Bible? Was it talked about in the Old Testament or just the New Testament? The answer is that it was talked about in both the Old Testament and the New Testament.

For example, in Exodus 19:5-6 (NKJV), God says to the Israelites, "Now therefore, if you will indeed obey My voice and keep My covenant, then you shall be a special treasure to Me above all people; for all the earth is Mine. 6 And you shall be to Me a kingdom of priests and a holy nation.' These are the words which you shall speak to the children of Israel."

God's form of government is a kingdom. Most people are familiar with earthly kingdoms, where there is a king, a queen, their royal subjects, citizens, ambassadors, governors, etc. But not too many are familiar with God's Kingdom, where He is the King supreme.

Unlike a democratic form of government or a republic, as King, God owns all of the territories that He governs over.

Psalms 89:11 (NLT) "The heavens are Yours, and the earth is Yours; everything in the world is Yours— You created it all."

The whole earth really belongs to God by virtue of the fact that He created it all.

Psalms 24:1 (NLT) backs this up by saying, "The earth is the Lord's, and everything in it. The world and all its people belong to Him."

Here is the problem. Sin came into the world when Adam and Eve sinned in the Garden of Eden. Therefore, the whole earth groans.

Romans 8:20-22 (NLT) says, "Against its will, all creation was subjected to God's curse. But with eager hope, 21 the creation looks forward to the day when it will join God's children in glorious freedom from death and decay. 22 For we know that all creation has been groaning as in the pains of childbirth right up to the present time."

People are groaning because they feel the effects of the curse in their lives in various ways, but they just don't know why they feel that way. So, God sent His Son Jesus Christ, born of a woman, to save all of mankind from their sins.

Matthew 1:18-23 (NLT) puts it this way, "This is how Jesus the Messiah was born. His mother, Mary, was engaged to be married to Joseph. But before the marriage took place, while she was still a virgin, she became pregnant through the power of the Holy Spirit. 19 Joseph, to whom she was engaged, was a righteous man and did not want to disgrace her publicly, so he decided to break the engagement quietly. 20 As he considered this, an angel of the Lord appeared to him in a dream. "Joseph, son of David," the angel said, "do not be afraid to take Mary as your wife. For the child within her was conceived by the Holy Spirit. 21 And she will have a Son, and you are to name Him Jesus, for He will save His people from their sins." 22 All of this occurred to fulfill the Lord's message through His prophet: 23 "Look! The virgin will conceive a child! She will give birth to a Son, and they will call Him Immanuel, which means 'God is with us.'"

The prophet Isaiah, under the inspiration of the Holy Spirit, wrote, Isaiah 9:6-7 (NKJV) "For unto us a Child is born, Unto us a Son is given; And the government will be upon His shoulder. And His name will be called Wonderful, Counselor, Mighty God, Everlasting Father, Prince of Peace. 7 Of the increase of His government and peace There will be no end, Upon the throne of David and over His kingdom, To order it and establish it with judgment and justice From that time forward, even forever. The zeal of the Lord of hosts will perform this."

Prophesied long before Jesus was born, we know that Jesus was to restore God's government in the earth as it was intended to be from the beginning of creation. Before mankind sinned, God's government ruled. After mankind sinned, a new demonic form of government ruled the earth, one that promoted destruction, murder, the pride of independence from God, and evil.

Nowhere do we read in the Old Testament or the New Testament that Jesus was establishing a new religion. God was always looking for a holy nation of His people that He could bless to replenish the earth, have dominion over it and rule it as His representatives in the earth. But to be the people that God wanted, mankind had to be made holy, righteous in His sight, have a heart for Him and follow Him. No matter how much mankind established its own religions and philosophical ideas, it could never meet God's conditions of holiness and righteous standards.

1 Peter 2:9-10 describes what God is looking for. It says, "But you are a chosen generation, a royal priesthood, a holy nation, His own special people, that you may proclaim the praises of Him who called you out of darkness into His marvelous light; 10 who once were not a people but are now the people of God, who had not obtained mercy but now have obtained mercy."

God is not only looking for a chosen generation but a people who are a royal priesthood, a holy nation, and His own special people. God is looking for a people who not only know His acts but know His ways. (Psalms 103:7).

Moses had the right idea when he said in Exodus 33:13-17, "Now therefore, I pray if I have found grace in Your sight, show me now Your way, that I may know You and that I may find grace in Your sight. And consider that this nation is Your people." 14 And He said, "My Presence will go with you, and I will give you rest." 15 Then he said to Him, "If Your Presence does not go with us, do not bring us up from here. 16 For how then will it be known that Your people and I have found grace in Your sight, except You go with us? So we shall be separate, Your people and I, from all the people who are upon the face of the earth." 17 So the Lord said to Moses, "I will also do this thing that you have spoken; for you have found grace in My sight, and I know you by name."

Let's look more in-depth at God's Kingdom government.

1) God's Kingdom government is to rule over His people in all areas of their lives. Scripture tells us in Matthew 4:17 (AMPC) how Jesus began His ministry. It says, "From that time Jesus began to preach, crying out, Repent (change your mind for the better, heartily amend your ways, with abhorrence of your past sins), for the Kingdom of Heaven is at hand." Jesus was ushering in God's grace.

Now, remember, every Law that was given in the Old Testament had a divine purpose behind it. The apostle Paul in his letter to the Galatians tells us what it is.

Galatians 3:19-26 (NLT) says, "Why, then, was the law given? It was given alongside the promise to show people their sins. But the law was designed to last only until the coming of the Child who was promised. God gave His law through angels to Moses, who was the mediator between God and the people. 20 Now a mediator is helpful if more than one party must reach an agreement. But God, who is One, did not use a mediator when He gave His promise to Abraham. 21 Is there a conflict, then, between God's law and God's promises? Absolutely not! If the law could give us new life, we could be made right with God by obeying it. 22 But the Scriptures declare that we are all prisoners of sin, so we receive God's promise of freedom only by believing in Jesus Christ. 23 Before the way of faith in Christ was available to us, we were placed under guard by the law. We were kept in protective custody, so to speak, until the way of faith was revealed. 24 Let me put it another way. The law was our guardian until Christ came; it protected us until we could be made right with God through faith. 25 And now that the way of faith has come, we no longer need the law as our guardian. 26 For you are all children of God through faith in Christ Jesus."

2) The Laws of God are perfect, eternal and good. (see also Psalms 19:6-9) Since all of God's laws are eternal and unchanging, even the laws in the Old Testament are eternal and good. Jesus commented on these eternal laws in Matthew 5:17-19 (AMPC) when He said, "Do not think that I have come to do away with or undo the Law or the Prophets; I have come not to do away with or undo but to complete and fulfill them. 18 For truly I tell you, until the sky and

earth pass away and perish, not one smallest letter nor one little hook [identifying certain Hebrew letters] will pass from the Law until all things [it foreshadows] are accomplished. 19 Whoever then breaks or does away with or relaxes one of the least [important] of these commandments and teaches men so shall be called least [important] in the Kingdom of Heaven, but he who practices them and teaches others to do so shall be called great in the Kingdom of Heaven."

These eternal laws are what govern Heaven and God's Kingdom on earth. These laws work whether we believe them or not, but they are the laws that are to govern the new man, not the old, natural man. When God says that we are to love our enemies and those who persecute us and despitefully use us, He is addressing how the new man is to live not the old man. People get on God for making their life miserable when they disobey. Yet, God is not directly making anyone's life miserable. All of God's laws come with consequences. Some bring blessings, and some bring curses. We can choose whether to obey God and His laws, but we have no choice in the consequences or outcome of our choices.

Therefore, God says to us in Galatians 6:7-8 "Do not be deceived, God is not mocked; for whatever a man sows, that he will also reap. 8 For he who sows to his flesh will of the flesh reap corruption, but he who sows to the Spirit will of the Spirit reap everlasting life." This is a divine Law, whether we believe it will work or not, and it is eternal.

Unfortunately, some people try to beat the divine laws of God because they are under the illusion that they can beat them. Even if a person beats man's justice, they cannot ever beat God's justice. Solomon, one of Israel's Kings, puts it this way when he said in Ecclesiastes 7:12 (NLT) "Wisdom and money can get you almost anything, but only wisdom can save your life." When it comes to divine justice, only the wisdom of God can save a person's life. A person cannot ever bribe God with anything. I always say, how can you bribe someone who owns it all?

Jesus tells us a lot in the Scripture about His Kingdom and how it works. For example, He says in Matthew 6:31-33, "Therefore do not worry, saying, 'What shall we eat?' or 'What shall we drink?' or 'What shall we wear?' 32 For after all these things the Gentiles seek. For your heavenly Father knows that you need all these things. 33 But seek first the kingdom of God and His righteousness, and all these things shall be added to you."

What is Jesus saying? I believe He is saying that when a person puts themselves under God's government, it is the same as putting themselves under the

Head of that government. We are not to worry because our King, i.e., Jesus Christ, will make sure that our needs are fully met when we believe. But we live in this world under the control of its system.

The head of the world's system is Satan. Many times, he will hinder our blessings from God. This is where an active faith in Jesus Christ comes in. To bring God's intended blessings towards us, we must exercise the faith of the new born again person of God.

In Luke 16:16 (AMPC) Jesus says, "Until John came, there were the Law and the Prophets; since then the good news (the Gospel) of the Kingdom of God is being preached, and everyone strives violently to go in [would force his own way rather than God's way into it]."

This means that up until John the Baptist, the Law and Prophets ruled to please God. However, since Jesus Christ, the Gospel is the means of God's grace, and it is the Gospel or Good News of the Kingdom of God. Many try to force their own way in, but none of that works. Why? Because the Gospel of the Kingdom of God stands upon faith in Jesus Christ. Anyone with another religion, philosophical idea or ideology that rejects Christ's Gospel will not inherit the Kingdom of God.

Matthew 7:13-14 (NLT) puts it this way, "You can enter God's Kingdom only through the narrow gate. The highway to hell is broad, and its gate is wide for the many who choose that way. 14 But the gateway to life is very narrow and the road is difficult, and only a few ever find it." Notice that the narrow gate is the gate to eternal life. Jesus clarifies that by saying in John 10:9 (NLT) "Yes, I am the gate. Those who come in through Me will be saved. They will come and go freely and will find good pastures." No religion, philosophy, or ideology gives its followers life. No Christ, no grace. No grace, no life. No Christ no freedom from sin and no narrow gate, just the broad one. Is this harsh? No, not if you seek the truth to eternal life.

3) Government is God-ordained. Just like marriage is God's institution, government is God's institution. Man may abuse it, just like the institution of marriage, but it still is God's institution. He is the only One qualified to determine how it is supposed to operate and what it means.

Romans 13:1-2 puts it this way, "Let every soul be subject to the governing authorities. For there is no authority except from God, and the authorities that exist are appointed by God. 2 Therefore whoever resists the authority resists the ordinance of God, and those who resist will bring judgment on themselves."

Jesus came to reestablish God's government on earth. As Daniel writes in Daniel 7:13-14 (NLT), "As my vision continued that night, I saw someone like a Son of Man coming with the clouds of Heaven. He approached the Ancient One and was led into His presence. 14 He was given authority, honor, and sovereignty over all the nations of the world, so that people of every race and nation and language would obey Him. His rule is eternal—it will never end. His kingdom will never be destroyed."

CHAPTER 2

WHY KNOWING ABOUT GOD'S GOVERNMENT IS IMPORTANT

I have found that when I didn't know the why of things, I tend to misrepresent them, and what people told me that I could do didn't seem to make real sense. For example, some people wonder why God doesn't just interfere in the lives of people, whether they want Him to or not. I had a person tell me many years ago, that the reason he does not serve God is that someone close to him died. God didn't answer his prayer for that person to live. I guess he figured that since God didn't answer his prayer the way he wanted it, he would rather be mad at God. But what if God did answer his prayer? I know with me that sometimes I want something so bad to happen one way, that anything contrary to what I believe is cast-off as not from God.

This also happens a lot denominationally. If a denomination doesn't believe in God a certain way, we go with what the denomination teaches rather than be open to what the Bible teaches. When this happens, everything that we read in Scripture is read through our denominational or religious lens. Therefore, I believe sometimes things are not taught that is in the Bible or are explained away. They don't fit with what we denominationally believe. Take God's government for an example. Though God is a God of government, many people assume that He is not. But I have found that when a person understands that God is a government God, then it helps them to understand God.

For example, many people believe that when Scripture says, "Thou shalt not kill or murder," that that applies to everything in God. They can't understand why a nation that believes in God would have a military that would go to war to protect itself from its enemies. Because after all, it says in the Bible that you shall not murder (Exodus 20:13). Yet, this does not apply to a nation and its military. Though there are laws that deal with person to person relationships (see Exodus 21:12), this is not the same as a nation going to war with another nation (Numbers 10:9).

As the nation of Israel went to war in 2 Chronicles 20, God was leading the fight. Also, a government must have some mechanism to punish evildoers and those who break its laws. If a government doesn't, then there will be nothing but chaos, confusion, and no justice for the innocent. But God is a God of justice, righteousness, truth, and order. King Nebuchadnezzar praised the government of God (Daniel 4:34) and even King Darius (Daniel 6:26). Yet, so many now think that they can dismiss God and His government as if it does not exist. The tiny nation of Israel still exists today, because of God's covenant with them, His government and His righteousness. Yet, God's enemies think that they can run roughshod over this tiny nation and take God's land away from them because of their strength. But God says differently (Deuteronomy 3:22; Deuteronomy 7:17-19).

Knowing about God's Kingdom government is important because it helps His people to understand who they are and what they must be about while living in this world. Think about it. Real dominion, authority, and power do not come about because of religious beliefs. It is a function of government.

When Jesus met a centurion in Capernaum (Matthew 8:5), he asked Jesus to come heal his servant. Jesus stated that He would come to his home to do just that. "The centurion answered and said, "Lord, I am not worthy that You should come under my roof. But only speak a word, and my servant will be healed. 9 For I also am a man under authority, having soldiers under me. And I say to this one, 'Go,' and he goes; and to another, 'Come,' and he comes; and to my servant, 'Do this,' and he does it." Matthew 8:8-9 (NKJV)

How could the centurion make this statement? Because of the governmental hierarchy of the Roman government. This extended to its military. This centurion had authority, rule, and dominion over his men when it came to government business. His superiors in Rome gave him this authority, as all Roman authority came from Caesar. The centurion had authority because he was under Caesar's authority. Satan has authority, power, a government, and governmental hierarchy. (Ephesians 6:12) It takes a government to defeat another government.

Matthew 8:10 says, "When Jesus heard it, He marveled, and said to those who followed, "Assuredly, I say to you, I have not found such great faith, not even in Israel!"

This centurion's faith was a product of his governmental authority over his men. The same can be said of the Christian's faith in God. Our authority and dominion over the earth is the result of God's government, i.e., our authority comes from His government. Just to say that someone has authority over the devil because of Jesus Christ is not really saying the whole truth. It is true that in Christ, we have authority and dominion, but that authority and rulership is backed by Christ's Kingdom government.

Therefore, there is a legal side to salvation, as well as a spiritual one. God's justice and judgments are legal entities. Jesus satisfied the claims of divine judgment by becoming the atoning sacrifice for the sins of the world. This happened, whether we believe it or not. The legal side says that there is also a governmental transfer of kingdoms or citizenship.

Colossians 1:13-14 (NLT) says, "For He has rescued us from the kingdom of darkness and transferred us into the Kingdom of His dear Son, 14 who purchased our freedom and forgave our sins."

This is not only spiritual but legal. The warfare that we Christians are involved in is between two governments. When Jesus was accused of casting out a demon by the power of Beelzebub by the Pharisees, Jesus said "...Every kingdom divided against itself is brought to desolation, and every city or house divided against itself will not stand (Matthew 12:25)." Then Jesus says in Matthew 12:26-28, "If Satan casts out Satan, he is divided against himself. How then will his kingdom stand? 27 And if I cast out demons by Beelzebub, by whom do your sons cast them out? Therefore they shall be your judges. 28 But if I cast out demons by the Spirit of God, surely the Kingdom of God has come upon you."

Here, we see a picture of warfare between two kingdoms, i.e., two governments. When two governments are at war with each other, if a person is a citizen of either of the two governments, they are automatically at war with the citizens of the other country. This is why Jesus says darkness hates light. Why? Because the kingdom of darkness is at war with the Kingdom of light.

Secondly, I believe the understanding of God's government brings synergy to the Gospel message, i.e., those who only look at the spiritual side of salvation and discipleship while ignoring the fact that there is also a legal side. Government includes the legal side of salvation as well. If one is just focusing on the spiritual side, then there are some things in the Bible that don't make sense. For example, if one looks at Matthew 6:33, it says, "But seek first the Kingdom of God and His righteousness, and all these things shall be added to you." When I was growing up, the preachers didn't fully explain this passage of

Scripture even though they quoted it. Many would tell me to seek Jesus first and not His Kingdom.

So, what is this verse saying? Jesus starts telling the crowd to not worry about their lives, what they would eat, drink or wear, and that worry would not change one's stature. Then Jesus says that the pagans worry about these things. He then says to seek God's Kingdom first, and His righteousness and all these things will be added. Matthew concludes by saying, "So don't worry about tomorrow, for tomorrow will bring its own worries. Today's trouble is enough for today (Matthew 6:34 NLT)."

When one becomes a citizen of a country, the government of that country is obligated to provide certain things for its citizens. In the Kingdom of God, the government will make sure that the citizen's needs are met. Just ask the King for what is needed in prayer, i.e., Matthew 6:11, "Give us this day our daily bread." Bread here comes from the Greek word "*artos*," meaning food, maintenance, living and necessities of life. Any government worth its salt is obligated to take care of its citizens. So, I believe Jesus is saying to seek God's government and God's way of making people in right standing with His government, and all needs will be provided.

Jesus demonstrated what Heaven's government was like every time He cast a demon out of someone, healed someone, or fed the multitudes (the 5000 and the 4000). He was demonstrating to the people the power of Heaven's government to meet all of their needs. When they repented of their sins and believed in Him for eternal life, the Father's government would meet their needs.

Do you believe this? Joshua 23:14 says, "…And you know in all your hearts and in all your souls that not one thing has failed of all the good things which the Lord your God spoke concerning you. All have come to pass for you; not one word of them has failed." (see also 1 Kings 8:56) This is still true today.

Remember, the government of Heaven is the Kingdom of Heaven. The Kingdom of Heaven includes the earth. The government of God on earth is the Kingdom of God. Knowing about the government of God is a powerful study because I believe it answers many questions that people have about God and His ways. Like why His people are a holy nation, with a government, a military, an economy, a culture, a values system, etc.

Knowing the fact that Jesus also came to restore God's government on earth will also help us to understand the Gospel better. The Gospel of God's

Kingdom prepares, equips, and causes people to focus on the things that are important in life.

Matthew 7:13-14 (NLT) says, "You can enter God's Kingdom only through the narrow gate. The highway to hell is broad, and its gate is wide for the many who choose that way. 14 But the gateway to life is very narrow and the road is difficult, and only a few ever find it." Yet, the world says that the broad road is the road to take because after all, all religions lead to the same end, right? Wrong! So, the question is, do you believe Jesus Christ or the world when it comes to your soul?

Remember, Jesus said, "What this world honors is detestable in the sight of God Luke 16:15b (NLT)." Putting the things of this world over God, loving this world and what it has to offer is going against God and what He stands for (1 John 2:15-16). So, how are we to live our lives? I believe we are to live our temporary lives here on earth in light of eternity. That is, this life must be lived as if eternity matters because this life will not only determine where we will spend eternity but also how we will spend eternity. We could say that this life actually prepares us for eternity.

Isn't it wonderful to know that God is a God of government? Think about it. Every religion, philosophy, or ideology is based upon a doctrine of beliefs.

Religions whether Christianity, Islam, Buddhism, Hinduism, Jehovah's Witness, Mormons, Judaism, New Age, Humanism, Baha'i, Taoism, Christian Science, Unitarianism, Wicca, Unification Church, etc. have a belief system or doctrine that they hold sacred. Yet, only Christianity has a legal side, not just a spiritual side. What does this mean?

Colossians 2:13-14 (NIV) puts it this way, "When you were dead in your sins and in the uncircumcision of your flesh, God made you alive with Christ. He forgave us all our sins, 14 having canceled the charge of our legal indebtedness, which stood against us and condemned us; He has taken it away, nailing it to the cross."

Legally, we deserved God's judgment of death, but Jesus Christ canceled all legal debt and charges against mankind, which condemned us and took it away, nailing it to the cross. And if there is no transference of kingdoms, all faiths would have the same end. But if one has a transference, where one goes from the kingdom of darkness to the kingdom of light, then its end is different from the rest. Each government only has the legal authority to lead and direct its own people. This is why a kingdom or government concept is important. This is not just about a belief system, but also about government.

Also note this. Countries have citizens. Only organizations have members, i.e., the local Church, Synagogues, Mosques, etc. Jesus said in John 3:17-18, "For God did not send His Son into the world to condemn the world, but that the world through Him might be saved. 18 "He who believes in Him is not condemned; but he who does not believe is condemned already, because he has not believed in the name of the only begotten Son of God."

That condemnation has to do with citizenship. The person who is not in the Kingdom of God is condemned. The word "already" implies that the kingdom a person is born into is not the Kingdom of God. That if they stay in that kingdom, they will be lost, no matter what they believe. When a person is a citizen of a country, their names and birth are on record with that country. As a result, they can obtain a passport from that country, stating that they are citizens of that country when they travel abroad. The Kingdom of God is no different. When a person is born again, their name is written in the Lambs Book of Life. If a person is not a citizen of the Kingdom of God, their name is not written in the Lambs Book of Life.

1 Timothy 4:1 says, "Now the Spirit expressly says that in later times some will depart from the faith, giving heed to deceiving spirits and doctrines of demons." This means that there are persons who were in the faith, and had their names written in the Lambs Book of Life. But when they departed from the faith, their names were deleted from this book.

Revelation 20:15 (NLT) picks this up by saying, "And anyone whose name was not found recorded in the Book of Life was thrown into the lake of fire." This can mean that a person whose name was not written in this Book, is now in there, or a person's name who was recorded in this Book is now no longer in it. If a person was a citizen of God's Kingdom through faith in Jesus Christ but is not any longer, they will be judged accordingly.

The prophet Ezekiel backs this up when God told him to write Ezekiel 18:24-28 (NLT) "However, if righteous people turn from their righteous behavior and start doing sinful things and act like other sinners, should they be allowed to live? No, of course not! All their righteous acts will be forgotten, and they will die for their sins. 25 "Yet you say, 'The Lord isn't doing what's right!' Listen to me, O people of Israel. Am I the one not doing what's right, or is it you? 26 When righteous people turn from their righteous behavior and start doing sinful things, they will die for it. Yes, they will die because of their sinful deeds. 27 And if wicked people turn from their wickedness, obey the law, and do what is just and right, they will save their lives. 28 They will live because they thought it over and decided to turn from their sins. Such people will not die."

Taken in context with God's grace, we turn from our wickedness when we come to God through faith in Jesus Christ. We fall from grace when we do what some Galatians did. Galatians 5:4 "You have become estranged from Christ, you who attempt to be justified by law; you have fallen from grace."

A person cannot ignore the Scripture and expect different results. I believe understanding God's government now is more critical than ever. Why? I believe it will not only affect the way we live in this life, but also how we live in this life. God wrote through the apostle Paul in 2 Corinthians 4:17-18 (AMPC), "For our light, momentary affliction (this slight distress of the passing hour) is ever more and more abundantly preparing and producing and achieving for us an everlasting weight of glory [beyond all measure, excessively surpassing all comparisons and all calculations, a vast and transcendent glory and blessedness never to cease!], 18 Since we consider and look not to the things that are seen but to the things that are unseen; for the things that are visible are temporal (brief and fleeting), but the things that are invisible are deathless and everlasting." We must now, more than ever, live this life now in light of our heavenly calling.

CHAPTER 3

WHAT IS THE GOSPEL OF THE KINGDOM?

Since the Gospel of the Kingdom is important to God, let us look at what it is and what it isn't. So many people have defined the Gospel or Good News of Jesus Christ as being about Him, not so much His Kingdom. But Luke 16:16 (AMPC) says, "Until John came, there were the Law and the Prophets; since then the good news (the Gospel) of the Kingdom of God is being preached, and everyone strives violently to go in [would force his own way rather than God's way into it]."

Just from reading this Scripture, we can see that what used to be about the Law and the Prophets is now about the Kingdom of God. This is what is to be preached now. Jesus also said in Matthew 6:33 (AMPC), "But seek (aim at and strive after) first of all His kingdom and His righteousness (His way of doing and being right), and then all these things taken together will be given you besides."

If I am to seek God's Kingdom first, then salvation must be about entering God's Kingdom. This being said, I can go to church, be very active doing religious work, be a professed Christian, and be outside of God's Kingdom.

Matthew 7:21-23 (NLT) says, "Not everyone who calls out to Me, 'Lord! Lord!' will enter the Kingdom of Heaven. Only those who actually do the will of My Father in Heaven will enter. 22 On judgment day many will say to Me, 'Lord! Lord! We prophesied in your name and cast out demons in your name and performed many miracles in your name.' 23 But I will reply, 'I never knew you. Get away from me, you who break God's laws.'"

This reminds me of Acts 8:11 (NIV) where it says, "They followed him because he had amazed them for a long time with his sorcery." The people called Simon "The great power of God." Yet, God was not in what he was doing. The real source of his power was Satan because all of the miracles of signs and wonders were actually done through sorcery or witchcraft. The people were fooled until they heard the real Gospel and saw the real power of God. Then they believed what Phillip preached concerning the Kingdom of God and name of Jesus Christ.

So, what is the Gospel of Jesus Christ?

1) It is a Gospel of grace not works. Man-made religions are all about works. Only God has a message of grace. Grace says that a person does not have to try to save themselves by keeping a bunch of rules and regulations. The pressure to do this can get to the point where you ask yourself, "Have I done enough to be saved?" The pressure to perform is taken away. Salvation depends upon people believing in Christ and in what He has done for us, not in our own deeds. The Good News is about entering God's Kingdom, where Jesus Christ provides a way for all people to enter through His shed blood.

Grace is God's invitation to enter His kingdom. The Law doesn't have anything to do with grace. It tells us how to live, but there is no power in it to help us to live what it says. This is what all false religions are based upon. Mankind can only concoct a religion of works, never of grace. Grace always comes from God to man, never from man to God. Within the confines of grace is the power to help us live right, according to God's standards. Yet, the grace that God offers mankind can only be received by faith, faith that only He gives. Grace is about living God's

Kingdom lifestyle with God's help. Even discipleship is about Kingdom living because living for God is nothing without living with God. In the Gospels, the twelve disciples lived with Jesus 24/7. This was a very important training concept in the Kingdom of God.

2) Salvation is now about entering the kingdom of God. Scriptures like Luke 1:2 (AMPC), "Exactly as they were handed down to us by those who from the [official] beginning [of Jesus' ministry] were eyewitnesses and ministers of the Word [that is, of the doctrine concerning the attainment through Christ of salvation in the Kingdom of God]," , and Luke 3:2 (AMPC), "In the high priesthood of Annas and Caiaphas, the Word of God [concerning the attainment through Christ of salvation in the Kingdom of God]…" are just some of the Scriptures that reveal to us what salvation involves. Those who refuse the message of Christ will not enter His Kingdom, thereby choosing the world and its Kingdom government over God's Kingdom government.

Colossians 1:13, 14 (NLT) tells us what that kingdom is. It says, "For He has rescued us from the kingdom of darkness and transferred us into the Kingdom of His dear Son, 14 who purchased our freedom and forgave our sins." Then Jesus says in John 3:3-6 "Jesus answered and said to him, "Most assuredly, I say to you, unless one is born again, he cannot see the Kingdom of God." 4 Nicodemus said to Him, "How can a man be born when he is old? Can he enter a second time into his mother's womb and be born?" 5 Jesus answered, "Most assuredly, I say to you, unless one is born of water and the Spirit, he cannot enter the Kingdom of God. 6 That which is born of the flesh is flesh, and that which is born of the Spirit is spirit." Even casting out demons is an open confrontation between God's Kingdom and Satan's (Matthew 12:22-29).

The only way to overcome an evil kingdom government is with another kingdom government that is good, yet not with a religious movement or belief system. The Good News is that Jesus Christ, the King of His government, defeated Satan and his government. We, the Church, must just enforce what Christ has already done.

Matthew 12:25-29, "But Jesus knew their thoughts, and said to them: "Every kingdom divided against itself is brought to desolation, and every city or house divided against itself will not stand. 26 If Satan casts out Satan, he is divided against himself. How then will his kingdom stand? 27 And if I cast out demons by Beelzebub, by whom do your sons cast them out? Therefore they shall be your judges. 28 But if I cast out demons by the Spirit of God, surely the kingdom of God has come upon you. 29 Or how can one enter a strong man's house and plunder his goods, unless he first binds the strong man? And then he will plunder his house."

Christianity puts people into God's Kingdom government as citizens. The apostle Paul wrote in Philippians 3:20, "For our citizenship is in Heaven, from which we also eagerly wait for the Savior, the Lord Jesus Christ," And Ephesians 2:19-20 "Now, therefore, you are no longer strangers and foreigners, but fellow citizens with the saints and members of the household of God, 20 having been built on the foundation of the apostles and prophets, Jesus Christ Himself being the chief cornerstone."

So, what is the Good News? It is that Jesus also opened the way for us Gentiles to be saved (See Ephesians 2:12). Before Christ, only the nation of Israel and any foreigner living under its rules had access to God's covenant promises. After Christ, the way is open for all people to be saved, i.e., both Jews and Gentiles. That is Good News!

3) **Salvation through faith in Jesus Christ and entering His kingdom is about possessing spiritual life.**

John 1:1-4 (AMPC) "IN THE beginning [before all time] was the Word (Christ), and the Word was with God, and the Word was God Himself. 2 He was present originally with God. 3 All things were made and came into existence through Him; and without Him was not even one thing made that has come into being. 4 In Him was Life, and the Life was the Light of men."

Also, 1 John 5:10-12 (NLT) says, "All who believe in the Son of God know in their hearts that this testimony is true. Those who don't believe this are actually calling God a liar because they don't believe what God has testified about His Son. 11 And this is what God has testified: He has given us eternal life, and this life is in His Son. 12 Whoever has the Son has life; whoever does not have God's Son does not have life."

Anyone who doesn't have the spirit of Christ does not belong to Him and therefore is not in the Kingdom of God or possesses eternal life.

4) **To enter the kingdom of God, the old man must die, and a new man must come into being with a total commitment to Jesus Christ.**

See also 2 Corinthians 5:17 & Matthew 16:24 - 26 (AMPC). Paul's letter to Titus puts it this way, Titus

3:4-7 (NLT), "But—When God our Savior, revealed His kindness and love, 5 He saved us, not because of the righteous things we had done, but because of His mercy. He washed away our sins, giving us a new birth and new life through the Holy Spirit. 6 He generously poured out the Spirit upon us through Jesus Christ our Savior. 7 Because of His grace He made us right in His sight and gave us confidence that we will inherit eternal life."

Since God's laws are eternal, they are meant to apply to the new man, not the old man. Yet, so many people try to keep them living through the old man and not the new. Remember, in the Kingdom of God; we are Christ's workmanship, Christ's masterpiece, i.e., a born-again new person. This is the person for whom God's laws are for. Yet, we are not to concentrate on following these laws. We concentrate on following the Holy Spirit. Jesus says in Ephesians 3:20, "Now to Him who is able to do exceedingly abundantly above all that we ask or think, according to the power that works in us."

Christ can do exceedingly abundantly above all that we ask or think, by the power that works within us. That power is the Person of the Holy Spirit. Christ works through the Holy Spirit within His new creations.

2 Timothy 1:9-10 (NLT) "For God saved us and called us to live a holy life. He did this, not because we deserved it, but because that was His plan from before the beginning of time—to show us His grace through Christ Jesus. 10 And now He has made all of this plain to us by the appearing of Christ Jesus, our Savior. He broke the power of death and illuminated the way to life and immortality through the Good News."

5) The Gospel of Jesus Christ reveals how Jesus broke the power of death for every human and illuminated the way to life and immortality.

Yet, only those who believe the Gospel of the Kingdom qualify to receive this display of grace. Remember, the Kingdom of Christ is all about freedom, eternal life, a brand new person, with a brand new purpose, etc.

6) God has pledged to meet the needs of those submitted to His government.

Matthew 6:31-34 (NLT) "So don't worry about these things, saying, 'What will we eat? What will we drink? What will we wear?' 32 These things dominate the thoughts of unbelievers, but your heavenly Father already knows all your needs. 33 Seek the Kingdom of God above all else, and live righteously, and he will give you everything you need. 34 "So don't worry about tomorrow, for tomorrow will bring its own worries. Today's trouble is enough for today. This is Good News.

Matthew 8:5-10 (NLT) "When Jesus returned to Capernaum, a Roman officer came and pleaded with Him, 6 "Lord, my young servant lies in bed, paralyzed and in terrible pain." 7 Jesus said, "I will come and heal him." 8 But the officer said, "Lord, I am not worthy to have You come into my home. Just say the word from where you are, and my servant will be healed. 9 I know this because I am under the authority of my superior officers, and I have authority over my soldiers. I only need to say, 'Go,' and they go, or 'Come,' and they come. And if I say to my slaves, 'Do this,' they do it." 10 When Jesus heard this, He was amazed. Turning to those who were following Him, He said, "I tell you the truth, I haven't seen faith like this in all Israel!" Because we are under the authority of Jesus Christ and His kingdom, we have authority in the earth.

7) Our authority and dominion over circumstances and satanic opposition come from being under authority to Christ and His kingdom.

When we exercise our authority and dominion, we are exercising our rights as Kingdom of God citizens. This is Good News, to know that we can control our circumstances and our lives to the glory of God. We can actually be above and not beneath regardless of our ethnic background. Hallelujah!!! (Also see Acts 16:16-34).

1 John 5:20 (NLT) "And we know that the Son of God has come, and He has given us understanding so that we can know the true God. And now we live in fellowship with the true God because we live in fellowship with His Son, Jesus Christ. He is the only true God, and He is eternal life." This is Good News! Why? **Because of Christ, we can know the true God and live in fellowship with Him.** An idol is not God. We can make an idol god to us, but an idol, something created by mankind, is not God. By believing the testimony of God concerning His Son Jesus, we receive the life of God, i.e., eternal life. As a result of Jesus, we can communicate with God directly. This is one of the privileges of being a citizen of God's Kingdom government.

8) When we, God's people represent God's kingdom, we represent God's government.

The Gospel of the Kingdom of God frees us to walk in complete freedom through Christ. Galatians

5:1 (AMPC), "IN [this] freedom Christ has made us free [and completely liberated us]; stand fast then, and do not be hampered and held ensnared and submit again to a yoke of slavery [which you have once put off]."

"(For the Lord is our Judge, The Lord is our Lawgiver, The Lord is our King; He will save us);" —Isaiah 33:22

God is government. He is interested in His people representing Him and His government. Dutch Sheets once said, that what God taught him about government was, "When the atmosphere is not right where we are, God has given His people authority to change it. Demonic unrest is Satan's government trying to take over the atmosphere where we are. We are to release the authority of the Lord over our many situations in life. A kingdom represents God's government, since He is King, Judge, and Lawgiver."[1] This is Good News. Remember the Good News or Gospel is about God's Kingdom government being available to humans through Jesus Christ and executed through Jesus Christ.

3

---

1 Dutch Sheets - God's Government Youtube Video Published on Mar 20, 2019

What is the gospel of Christ?

The apostle Paul writes in Galatians 1:6-8, "I marvel that you are turning away so soon from Him who called you in the grace of Christ, to a different gospel, 7 which is not another; but there are some who trouble you and want to pervert the gospel of Christ. 8 But even if we, or an angel from Heaven, preach any other gospel to you than what we have preached to you, let him be accursed."

Matthew 4:23, "And Jesus went about all Galilee, teaching in their synagogues, preaching the gospel of the Kingdom, and healing all kinds of sickness and all kinds of disease among the people."

Mark 1:14-15, "Now after John was put in prison, Jesus came to Galilee, preaching the gospel of the Kingdom of God, 15 and saying, "The time is fulfilled, and the Kingdom of God is at hand. Repent, and believe in the gospel."

The gospel of Christ is the gospel of the Kingdom.

To preach Jesus Christ, one must mention His kingdom. Acts 8:12, "But when they believed Philip as he preached the things concerning the Kingdom of God and the name of Jesus Christ, both men and women were baptized."

Acts 19:8, "And he (Paul) went into the synagogue and spoke boldly for three months, reasoning and persuading concerning the things of the Kingdom of God."

Acts 20:24-27, "But none of these things move me; nor do I count my life dear to myself, so that I may finish my race with joy, and the ministry which I received from the Lord Jesus, to testify to the gospel of the grace of God. 25 "And indeed, now I know that you all, among whom I have gone preaching the kingdom of God, will see my face no more. 26 Therefore I testify to you this day that I am innocent of the blood of all men. 27 For I have not shunned to declare to you the whole counsel of God."

Are we preaching the whole counsel of God or a part of it, giving the impression that it is the whole counsel of God?

Since there is no sickness in Heaven, since there is no lack or shortage in Heaven, and since there is no sin in Heaven, then Jesus has given people a taste of what it would be like in Heaven. Jesus fed the multitudes and paid the disciple's taxes to let them know that there is no lack or shortage in Heaven. Jesus preached the Gospel of the Kingdom to let the people know that obedience to His gospel was not the same as obedience to a religion. That there was power released into a person's life as a result of obedience to the true Gospel. That there were spirit and life in Jesus' Words. Scripture not only tells us where we are now, but it corrects us and gives us hope of what could be if we believe in the Son of Man, Jesus Christ, as Lord and Savior.

God's Word separates the wheat from the tares, the wheat from the chaff, the good from evil and heaven's perspective contrasted with the perspective of the world. The Word of God shows us what a person can be and do if they learn to wait upon the Lord and allow Him to prepare them.

As long as the disciples followed Jesus, they got first-hand evidence of what it would be like in God's Kingdom.

The laws and precepts of God also give first-hand knowledge of what it is like to live in God's kingdom. Without the Word of God, there can be no repentance. God wants us to walk with Him daily because every day, we must make decisions, and if a person doesn't stay attuned to God, they will veer off away from God. (See Psalm 106:13-15).

Here is a side note: **Why is the life we are living now important?** Because we have to enter God's kingdom now, before we physically die, in order to live in His Kingdom after we die. If we die as citizens of the kingdom of Satan, then we will spend eternity in hell, which will eventually go to the lake of fire, because that is where that kingdom is destined. So, this life is really to prepare us for the life to come. Unfortunately, too many can't see this and so put great emphasis on this temporary life, at the expense of the never-ending life after physical death. God showed me one day that living in this life seems so very real now, and the afterlife seems unreal. But when we die, the afterlife becomes real and this temporary life, the one that we are living in now, will seem unreal. It is almost like going on a beautiful vacation. While on vacation, home seems like a distant memory. But when you come home, the vacation seems like a distant memory. As the years go by, the vacation fades more and more into the distant past, such that if it wasn't for photographs or videos, much of it would be lost in our conscience minds.

DISCIPLESHIP

I believe discipleship is a very important part of the Gospel of the Kingdom that so many times it is overlooked. I mentioned to some people a while back, what happens if you get saved or enter God's Kingdom at age 10 but don't die until age 80. What are you to do between the ages of 10 and 80?

Answer: Learn what it means to be a disciple of Christ and then walk in it.

Question: How does the kingdom of God answer the question of discipleship? After all, Jesus tells us in Matthew 28:19, "Go therefore and make disciples of all the nations, baptizing them in the name of the Father and of the Son and of the Holy Spirit," But, Jesus, how do we do this?

Matthew 28:20 (NLT), "Teach these new disciples to obey all the commands I have given you. And be sure of this: I am with you always, even to the end of the age." We do it by relying upon two things.

1) We learn and obey God's commands, and 2) We always rely on Jesus being with us personally, and corporately helping us. What do these commands deal with? Good works, i.e., who we are in Christ, purpose, assignment, following Christ, discerning between what is of Christ and what is not of Christ, and fulfilling one's destiny to name a few things. According to Dr. Myles Munroe, there are five questions that every person asks themselves, whether they ask out loud or silently to themselves. They are:

Who am I? (which deals with Identity)
Where am I from? (which deals with Heritage)
Why am I here? (which deals with Purpose)
What can I do? (which deals with Potential)
Where am I going? (which deals with Hope)[2]

The Good News of the Kingdom addresses all of these questions and more. This is why discipleship is so important. Discipleship is where we can learn to walk in the benefits of being in God's Kingdom. Discipleship is where we learn to use the keys of the Kingdom of Heaven, as mentioned in Matthew 16:19. We as humans need to know, understand, and apply God's principles in order for us to reach our full potential as human beings. When one accepts the Lord Jesus Christ into their lives, they are at the baby stage of their spiritual life. Now, they must grow and mature. The process and complexity of this spiritual journey are attainable only through a living faith in the Lord Jesus Christ. God puts it this way:

Ephesians 2:10 (NLT), "For we are God's masterpiece. He has created us anew in Christ Jesus, so we can do the good things He planned for us long ago."
4

---

[2] Myles Munroe Youtube video, "Understanding the Meaning for Your Existence" Published on June 21, 2017

Everything that we are in Christ, everything that we are to do in Christ, and all of our past, present, and future can be answered and experienced in Christ. So, when "Jesus said to the people who believed in Him, "You are truly My disciples if you remain faithful to My teachings. 32 And you will know the truth, and the truth will set you free." (John 8:31, 32 NLT), He was saying that faithfulness in the long term, not short term, leads to a life of long term freedom. One's intimate knowledge of and personal experience of Jesus Christ, Who embodies Truth, leads one to full freedom.

"For the law of the Spirit of life [which is] in Christ Jesus [the law of our new being] has freed me from the law of sin and of death." (Romans 8:2 AMPC)

CHAPTER 4

IS THE GOSPEL OF THE KINGDOM RELEVANT FOR TODAY?

Jesus made an important statement in Matthew 5:17-18 (NLT), "Don't misunderstand why I have come. I did not come to abolish the law of Moses or the writings of the prophets. No, I came to accomplish their purpose. 18 I tell you the truth, until Heaven and earth disappear, not even the smallest detail of God's law will disappear until its purpose is achieved." This is backed up in Luke 16:17 (NLT), "But that doesn't mean that the law has lost its force. It is easier for Heaven and earth to disappear than for the smallest point of God's law to be overturned."

God's precepts and laws are forever binding. As the Psalmist says in Psalm 119:89, "Forever, O Lord,

Your Word is settled in Heaven." Since God's Word is eternal, it still applies today and into the future. The Word of God's Kingdom government is the only message that Jesus came to bring all people. Since the dispensation of grace began on the day of Pentecost, people today are still responsible for deciding whether to accept God's grace or not. How many times have you heard people say that they have outgrown God today? Or that today since mankind has more knowledge than ever before, we as humans don't need God anymore. Yet, what I hear and see happening all around me, refutes this logic. People are still born in sin. People are still bound by sin in their lives. People are still committing suicide, murdering others, living immoral lives, still not knowing why they are here, still being manipulated by greed, material things, falling under the pressure and stress to be true to themselves, etc. In other words, people are still being people, regardless of ethnicity or culture.

Jesus puts it succinctly when He says in 1 Corinthians 1:19-21 (NLT), "As the Scriptures say, "I will destroy the wisdom of the wise and discard the intelligence of the intelligent." 20 So where does this leave the philosophers, the scholars, and the world's brilliant debaters? God has made the wisdom of this world look foolish. 21 Since God in His wisdom saw to it that the world would never know Him through human wisdom, He has used our foolish preaching to save those who believe."

Then He says in 1 Corinthians 1:27-29 (NLT) "... God chose things the world considers foolish in order to shame those who think they are wise. And He chose things that are powerless to shame those who are powerful. 28 God chose things despised by the world, things counted as nothing at all, and used them to bring to nothing what the world considers important. 29 As a result, no one can ever boast in the presence of God."

I don't know what anyone else thinks, but for God to do this, is a minuscule display of His power. Remember, God doesn't just call us to be saved from the corruption that is in the world (2 Peter 1:4), but He calls for us to live our new lives in Him and for Him. Hence, we are called to be disciples. Because of the Kingdom of God's mandate, we each have a divine work to do. Some are called to fulfill Ephesians 4:11-12 (NLT) which says, "Now these are the gifts Christ gave to the church: the apostles, the prophets, the evangelists, and the pastors and teachers. 12 Their responsibility is to equip God's people to do His work and build up the church, the body of Christ."

Some are called to be deacons (1 Timothy 3:8); others have gifts mentioned in Romans 12:4 - 8. A gift is to be used for the glory of God. Kingdom leadership is the leadership that uses the gifts that God has given them for His glory.

Is living in the Kingdom of God relevant for today?

You bet it is. Why? Because the kingdom of God works in any environment, situation, or setting. The Kingdom of God works in any marketplace. The Kingdom of God has a solution for every earthly problem. Remember, Jesus told His disciples in Matthew 10:1 "And when He had called His twelve disciples to Him, He gave them power over unclean spirits, to cast them out, and to heal all kinds of sickness and all kinds of disease."

Then it says in Matthew 10:7-14, "And as you go, preach, saying, The Kingdom of Heaven is at hand.' 8 Heal the sick, cleanse the lepers, raise the dead, cast out demons. Freely you have received, freely give. 9 Provide neither gold nor silver nor copper in your money belts, 10 nor bag for your journey, nor two tunics, nor sandals, nor staffs; for a worker is worthy of his food. 11 "Now whatever city or town you enter, inquire who in it is worthy, and stay there till you go out. 12 And when you go into a household, greet it. 13 If the household is worthy, let your peace come upon it. But if it is not worthy, let your peace return to you.

14 And whoever will not receive you nor hear your words, when you depart from that house or city, shake off the dust from your feet."

Here, we see that God's Kingdom government is also practical. God's Kingdom message gives people control of their lives again. It gives them a sense of purpose because we each have a God-given assignment given to us by God that is bigger than ourselves. Once in God's Kingdom, we each can make significant contributions to the society and generation that we live in, that also has eternal value and reward. The good works mentioned in Ephesians 2:10 and 2 Timothy 3:17 include this.

Romans 14:17 (NLT) then says, "For the Kingdom of God is not a matter of what we eat or drink, but of living a life of goodness and peace and joy in the Holy Spirit."

We are to live our lives by and through the power of the Holy Spirit to live in the Kingdom of God as intended. Translated, this means that to stay connected and close to God, we must receive revelation from God and the ability to handle any earthly problem that we face, with God's help. We can pray to God and receive the ability to solve problems, face opposition, never lose hope or become discouraged and even be the head and not the tail in every endeavor that God allows us to undertake.

Just like Jesus was never at a loss for anything that came His way, we can rely on our Father as well. Except that we do it in Jesus' name. In the USA, because the Church system wants to be accepted by the world's system, I believe we, the Church, actually hinder God from doing all that He wants done in our cultures. Too many times, I believe that we become part of the problem, rather than solutions to the problems that our country faces. Too many of us don't really hear what the Father is saying on too many issues.

So, we echo the world's response. Yet, because we are citizens of the Kingdom of Heaven, God is merciful towards giving His Church, His ecclesia, another chance.

Another reason the Kingdom of God is relevant is that mankind lives under two kingdoms or two governments, i.e., the seen and unseen, or the visible and the invisible. The visible government is what a person is living under in their country. The invisible or unseen government is the government they live under spiritually. There are only two unseen governments, no matter what man says — the kingdom of Satan or the Kingdom of Jesus Christ. The way into the kingdom of Satan is through the wide gate. The way into the Kingdom of Jesus Christ is through the narrow gate. Why? Because of Acts 4:11-12 (NIV) which says, "Jesus is "the stone you builders rejected, which has become the cornerstone.' 12 Salvation is found in no one else, for there is no other name under heaven given to mankind by which we must be saved."

The unseen government rules the seen government. In other words, the unseen government of Satan can put pressure on people to conform to his will. Only the unseen government of God, through Jesus Christ, can counter and ultimately defeat Satan and his government.

I believe that in some instances, what holds God back from doing more has to do with His Church. By our actions or inactions, we give the false impression to the world that God is not who He says He is. This is addressed in 1 Corinthians 4:19-20 (NET) which says, "But I will come to you soon, if the Lord is willing, and I will find out not only the talk of these arrogant people, but also their power. 20 For the Kingdom of God is demonstrated not in idle talk but with power." I believe that God's power has more to do than just with healing the sick or delving into the prophetic. I believe that it also includes things like solving all human problems, from political issues to social issues, from financial issues to family issues, issues of crime, religion, and the like. Since Jesus is the answer, then He is the answer to all human problems, not just some.

But, He will not force Himself on anyone who doesn't want Him or believe in Him. Jesus' Good News is unfortunately not received by everyone, though it really is what they are looking for. What do I mean by that? I mean if someone is looking for world peace, Jesus is the answer. If they are looking for control of their destiny, Jesus is the answer. If they are looking for utopia or a heaven, Jesus is the answer. If they are searching for identity, purpose, heritage, finding their calling or a reason to live, Jesus is the answer. If someone needs deliverance from bondage, hate, bitterness, shame, low self-esteem, lack, sickness, whether mental or physical, or disease, Jesus is the answer. The Gospel of Jesus Christ is relevant for today because people are experiencing all of these issues. Yet, with God, one cannot manipulate Him or shame Him into doing something for them. He only responds to exercising one's faith in some capacity.

Hebrews 11:6 (AMPC) puts it this way, "But without faith it is impossible to please and be satisfactory to Him. For whoever would come near to God must [necessarily] believe that God exists and that He is the rewarder of those who earnestly and diligently seek Him [out]."

Then Jesus says in John 6:37 (AMPC) "All whom My Father gives (entrusts) to Me will come to Me; and the one who comes to Me I will most certainly not cast out [I will never, no never, reject one of them who comes to Me]."

To summarize, this Gospel of the Kingdom of God is as relevant today as it was when Jesus walked the earth. God is so good! If you don't know Jesus Christ as your Lord and Savior, then repeat this prayer after me once you are sincere and meet the conditions of Hebrews 11:6 and Romans 10:9, 10.

"God, I am coming to You because I believe that You exist, though I may not know Your name. I come honestly, sincerely, and openly. You are right. I do need a Savior. I agree with You. I repent of my sins, and I am sorry for the wrong that I have done. I ask You for Your forgiveness. I ask You to save me from this world's corruption, and I believe in my heart that You died for me, died to take away my sins and iniquities. I ask You to make me a brand-new person, with a brand-new heart. Fill me with Your Holy Spirit, in Jesus' name, Amen."

CHAPTER 5

FULFILLING ONES DESTINY

2 Timothy 1:8-9 "God, 9 Who has saved us and called us with a holy calling, not according to our works, but according to His own purpose and grace which was given to us in Christ Jesus before time began."

In the Kingdom of God, we find that Jesus not only saved us, but He has called us with a holy calling and a specific purpose to fulfill a measure of the grace that He has given us. According to Ephesians 4:16 (NLT), Jesus "makes the whole body fit together perfectly. As each part does its own special work, it helps the other parts grow, so that the whole body is healthy and growing and full of love." Romans 12:6a (AMPC) says, "Having gifts (faculties, talents, qualities) that differ according to the grace given us, let us use them."

Here, we see that Christ has given mankind the following: 1) Salvation through faith in Jesus Christ. 2) Each person their own special work that is designed to complement and help the rest of the body of Christ so that the body is healthy and growing and full of love, and 3) Gifts that reflect the measure of grace given to us by God for the work of ministry. In other words, what God has for each of us to do cannot be done until after we have been made new creations in Christ Jesus. Then and only then can we do the good works that we are called to. But, remember, we are called to them before we are saved.

Too many people look at calling as something like an apostle, a prophet, an evangelist, a pastor, a teacher, or a deacon, etc. But each of us is called to a special work, and not all of us are called to a church ministry. Some of us must then have, what we call, a marketplace ministry. That is, to fulfill our calling means that we must, at least, finish that work, the work of marketplace ministry, in order to finish our race here on earth. Many in the church die, and in their obituary, all that is mentioned are birth dates, parents names, kids if any, names with or without spouses, maybe some close relatives, where a person went to school, and what positions, if any, that were held at church. But very little, if any, about their calling. Most talk about the deceased from a purely human point of view, that they were a good person, a good friend, a lovely family member, etc., but nothing about calling. Yet, Scripture tells us in 2 Timothy 4:6-7 where the apostle Paul wrote, "For I am already being poured out as a drink offering, and the time of my departure is at hand. 7 I have fought the good fight, I have finished the race, I have kept the faith."

To finish the race that we are created by God to run, we must accomplish our calling. Our calling is as vital to do and finish as any other church ministry. Most people have no idea what their calling is, let alone finish it. But everything that God creates has a purpose. The mountains have a purpose. The oxen have a purpose. The lions have a purpose. The gold and the silver have a purpose. Science has a purpose. History has a purpose, and even humans have a purpose. Yet, how to fulfill that purpose rests in God.

God says in Ecclesiastes 3:11 (AMPC) "He has made everything beautiful in its time. He also has planted eternity in men's hearts and minds [a divinely implanted sense of a purpose working through the ages which nothing under the sun but God alone can satisfy], yet so that men cannot find out what God has done from the beginning to the end." To put it bluntly, everything that God has given mankind is tied to his or her divine purpose and destiny. The fulfilling of our purpose and the finishing of our divine destiny on earth has eternal consequences and value.

Unfortunately, too many think that having a divine destiny limits their life. They want to be free to choose their own destiny. But God says in Deuteronomy 30:19 (NLT), "Today I have given you the choice between life and death, between blessings and curses. Now I call on Heaven and earth to witness the choice you make. Oh, that you would choose life, so that you and your descendants might live!"

Then in 1 John 5:11-12 (NLT) God says, "And this is what God has testified: He has given us eternal life, and this life is in His Son. 12 Whoever has the Son has life; whoever does not have God's Son does not have life." So, God has given each person a free choice. We are all free to choose God's way or another way. But we are not free to choose the consequences that each decision carries. That belongs to God. We can choose to be vessels of honor or vessels of dishonor, but we cannot be both. Some people know at an early age what they want to do with their lives when they come of age. But they still can't gravitate to their calling until they are born again and living for the Lord Jesus Christ.

So, how does one know of or discover their divine calling? I can only give you what I have learned firsthand from the Scriptures and my experience. Just like there are various gifts of the Spirit, various ministries from Jesus and various operations of how each ministry is to work from God the Father, there are some similarities and some differences for each person. Here is what I know.

A person must first be in the kingdom of God.

Why? Because one's calling is for the new man in Christ, not the old man. It's like trying to put new wine into old wineskins. It won't work. It's like what God says in Ephesians 2:10 (NLT) "For we are God's masterpiece. He has created us anew in Christ Jesus, so we can do the good things He planned for us long ago."

A person must live a godly life.

God warns us through the apostle Paul that there are people who "will act religious, but they will reject the power that could make them godly. Stay away from people like that!" —2 Timothy 3:5 (NLT)

With a Godly life, we must have a strong desire to do what God wants us to do. There must be a hunger. If there is no hunger, there is no motivation to know.

Unfortunately, there are too many who don't know, are not looking to know, and have just settled for being just a bench member of the local church, maybe doing a few small tasks, but basically, just blending in with the crowd. Then, some settle for doing things that they are qualified for in the secular world only. So, if they are a teacher in secular society, they try to bring that into the church and only do that. If they are an accountant, they do that for the church, and so on. But part of a godly lifestyle is seeking to find your niche in the body of Christ.

The only qualified Person to reveal one's divine calling is God.

It could come through prophesy, directly, a dream, a vision or inner witness. But God will communicate to you your calling in some capacity. I remember years ago when I was in the US Air Force; I was grounded from being an aircrew member right after graduation from navigation school. It was discovered that I had a 2nd degree AV block in my heart by the medical staff at the base where I was stationed. When I was flown to Brooks AFB in Texas, I underwent very rigorous testing to get a better picture of the severity of the problem. While at Brooks AFB, I had an encounter with God, Who kept reminding me that He had called me into the ministry. I didn't want to do it. I told Him no. We had a wrestling, as He wouldn't let me sleep until I agreed to potentially do what He wanted. I conceded, and He then allowed me to go to sleep. God wanted me to preach, and I just didn't want to do that. God allowed me run for a while longer until things came to a head when I was stationed in Maine. I had to decide to do His will or not. To make a long story short, I submitted to Him, because that was my heart's desire, though I thought I should do something else. Though there have been some rough patches, that was the best decision I ever made, followed by discovering with whom to marry. But it was God who directed me into my calling, not man. And by following God, He verified to other people that what I was doing was His will.

Sometimes, God lets us know about our assignment while we are young, though we don't know all the details. As I mentioned earlier, some people know early in life about their calling. But what they don't know are the details of it. Sometimes, because we don't know the details, as we get older, we start directing our own path to accomplish the calling. That is a mistake. Why? Because of Galatians 4:22-23 (NLT), "The Scriptures say that Abraham had two sons, one from his slave wife and one from his freeborn wife. 23 The son of the slave wife was born in a human attempt to bring about the fulfillment of God's promise. But the son of the freeborn wife was born as God's own fulfillment of His promise."

When we do what we think, we get Ishmael. When we allow God to fulfill His own promise to us, we get Isaac. Jesus says in John 6:63 (NLT) that, "Human effort accomplishes nothing." When we try to make our own careers, build our own empires, we are doing it and not God. Some reach their pinnacle of success and still feel empty inside. Others, who have more callous hearts, just use that feeling to accomplish more and more and more on their own. They don't realize that human effort accomplishes nothing for them eternally. They don't realize that God not only must give us the vision, but He must carry out the vision through them, and the vision must bring Him glory.

Romans 11:36 (AMPC) puts it this way, "For from Him and through Him and to Him are all things. [For all things originate with Him and come from Him; all things live through Him, and all things center in and tend to consummate and to end in Him.] To Him be glory forever! Amen (so be it)."

Then Philippians 2:13 (AMPC) says, "[Not in your own strength] for it is God Who is all the while effectually at work in you [energizing and creating in you the power and desire], both to will and to work for His good pleasure and satisfaction and delight."

Remember, just because God puts our calling and assignments in our hearts as kids, that doesn't mean that we will do them, or make them our aim when we get older. An awful lot of people choose a career and allow the work or calling of God to fall by the wayside, which we can do by choice. However, God makes it clear that since He is the definition of good, then anything outside of Him is evil. Since Jesus is the light of the world, anything outside of Christ is in the dark. For darkness is defined as the absence of light. Error and lies are defined as the absence of truth. We each have a choice to do God's good works or not. But as Kingdom citizens, we are expected to fulfill our calling and assignment. Why? Because that is part of the good works that we are to do as a result of being in God's Kingdom.

CHAPTER 6

FINAL THOUGHTS ON THE KINGDOM OF GOD

1 Corinthians 4:20, "For the kingdom of God is not in word but in power."

This is a very powerful concept, that can be overlooked if we are not careful. Where there is no power being manifested that glorifies God, then the Kingdom is either not there or is dormant and not being demonstrated by God's people. Many times, it is the religion of Christianity that is on the job, at the store or among the people and not the Kingdom of God. I am differentiating between the religion of Christianity and Christianity as defined by the Bible. In the Bible, the Kingdom of God represents true Christianity.

The religion of Christianity is a system that has been invented by man to take the place of the

Kingdom of God. In many local churches, the religion of Christianity has replaced the Kingdom of God, and the sad part is that many do not know it. They are so used to organized religion, that even when the Holy Spirit moves, they want to shut it down.

It reminds me of Luke 8:35-37 (NIV), "and the people went out to see what had happened. When they came to Jesus, they found the man from whom the demons had gone out, sitting at Jesus' feet, dressed and in his right mind; and they were afraid. 36 Those who had seen it told the people how the demon-possessed man had been cured. 37 Then all the people of the region of the Gerasenes asked Jesus to leave them, because they were overcome with fear. So He got into the boat and left."

Even the apostle Paul said in Galatians 1:6-9, "I marvel that you are turning away so soon from Him who called you in the grace of Christ, to a different gospel, 7 which is not another; but there are some who trouble you and want to pervert the gospel of Christ. 8 But even if we, or an angel from Heaven, preach any other gospel to you than what we have preached to you, let him be accursed. 9 As we have said before, so now I say again, if anyone preaches any other gospel to you than what you have received, let him be accursed."

So, a false grace is preached, a religion of Christianity in many cases takes precedence over the Kingdom of God, and not to mention a counterfeit faith.

Scripture tells us where the Kingdom of God is; among God's people. Luke 17:20-21 (AMPC) "Asked by the Pharisees when the Kingdom of God would come, He replied to them by saying, The Kingdom of God does not come with signs to be observed or with visible display, 21 Nor will people say, Look! Here [it is]! or, See, [it is] there! For behold, the Kingdom of God is within you [in your hearts] and among you [surrounding you]."

I mentioned earlier that a person can be a member of a church, be a regular attendant, and still miss the Kingdom of God because real salvation is about entering the Kingdom of God (See Luke 1:2 AMPC). People who practice religion can take God's Word and change it to fit its beliefs and feel that it is OK to do so, not realizing that all Scripture is God-breathed. Anything or anyone who attempts to alter it adulterates it because it no longer has the breath of God on it. It may sound good, but it is misleading and false. Anything that attempts to lead people away from the Kingdom of God is false, though it may be religious.

Sometimes, people put so much emphasis on preaching, that they do what Paul said not to do. The apostle Paul wrote, "And my message and my preaching were very plain. Rather than using clever and persuasive speeches, I relied only on the power of the Holy Spirit. 5 I did this so you would trust not in human wisdom but in the power of God." --(1 Corinthians 2:4-5 NLT).

Too many preachers rely on clever phrases and rhetoric to persuade people about Jesus, rather than relying upon the Holy Spirit to not only give them what to say but also to help them deliver God's message. But nothing that man has can do what the power of the Holy Spirit can do. People want to hear God, not clever and persuasive messages. Remember, the Kingdom of God is not in talk but in power. The kind of power and supernatural ability that God is talking about is of the Holy Spirit. Too many people caught up in the occult get their power from Satan. One does not have to call themselves a Satanist to get their power from Satan. Witchcraft gets its power from Satan along with witches, whether a good one or a bad one, it doesn't matter. Yoga, transcendental meditation, paranormal, wizardry, fortune telling, crystal balls, mediums, familiar spirits, etc., are all not of God but of the world. Remember, the world's system gets its power and influence from Satan (2 Corinthians 4:4).

Ephesians 2:1-2 (AMPC) says, "…you were dead (slain) by [your] trespasses and sins 2 In which at one time you walked [habitually]. You were following the course and fashion of this world [were under the sway of the tendency of this present age], following the prince of the power of the air. [You were obedient to and under the control of] the [demon] spirit that still constantly works in the sons of disobedience [the careless, the rebellious, and the unbelieving, who go against the purposes of God]."

Therefore, it takes power and force to overcome the strongman and to overcome all the power of the enemy.

Remember, the kingdom of God is in power. So:
- Salvation is a work of God's power (John 1:12).
- Being filled with the Holy Spirit is a work of God's power (Acts 1:8).
- Discipleship and Godly living are a work of God's power (Ephesians 6:10; 2 Timothy 3:5 NLT).
- Walking with God requires power (Matthew 22:29; 2 Corinthians 13:4).
- Accomplishing one's divine assignment requires power (Matthew 10:1, Mark 16:20; Luke 9:1).

- The grace of God displays God's power (2 Corinthians 12:9; Ephesians 3:7).
- Jesus Christ is God's power (Romans 1:4; 1 Corinthians 1:24).
- The Gospel Message is a representation of God's power (Romans 1:16; 1 Corinthians 1:18).

This list could go on and on. To minister the Kingdom of God to others requires ministering in the power of God's Kingdom as His representative. Jesus Christ taught in the authority and power of God and ministered in God's power when He taught, preached, healed the sick, raised the dead and fed multitudes of people. Yet, a manifestation of this power in humans is really a gift from God, received and acted upon by faith. Anything that does not come from God does not require His faith to act on it. But anything that does come from God must be activated by His faith for it to please Him.

This concept of the Kingdom of Heaven and the Kingdom of God affected my life and faith in a very significant way. How? As a serious student and follower of Jesus Christ, there was a lack of understanding as to the why of things. For an example, in Isaiah 9:6-7, it says, "For unto us a Child is born, Unto us a Son is given; And the government will be upon His shoulder. And His name will be called Wonderful,

Counselor, Mighty God, Everlasting Father, Prince of Peace. Of the increase of His government and peace There will be no end, Upon the throne of David and over His kingdom, To order it and establish it with judgment and justice From that time forward, even forever. The zeal of the Lord of hosts will perform this."

I did not understand what God meant when He said that the government would be upon Jesus' shoulder. What government? Then in verse seven, it says, "Of the increase of His government and peace there would be no end…". Again, the question was, what government? Jesus was to be upon the throne of David and over His Kingdom. Why? When Jesus said to seek the Kingdom of God and His righteousness, Matthew 6:33, I did not understand. But the concept of God having and introducing His government on the earth answered a lot of questions. The problem was that there was not enough information on God's government, and I found that so many Christians, not only didn't understand it themselves, but many didn't understand how it fits in with the Gospel message that was being preached by many Christian ministers.

Then, one day, I heard a message from the late Dr. Myles Munroe, and this piqued my interest. So, I bought and read two of his books[1] on the subject and then I asked the Lord to directly teach me about His government so that I would have personal experience with it.

He has been doing that, and I have been gaining experience and wisdom about His Kingdom government.

In conclusion, **The gift of God's grace includes:**

Salvation in the Kingdom of God

Luke 1:2 (AMPC), "Exactly as they were handed down to us by those who from the [official] beginning [of Jesus' ministry] were eyewitnesses and ministers of the Word [that is, of the doctrine concerning the attainment through Christ of salvation in the Kingdom of God]," (Also Romans 6:23).

Being filled with the Holy Spirit

Acts 2:38 (AMPC), "And Peter answered them, Repent (change your views and purpose to accept the will of God in your inner selves instead of rejecting it) and be baptized, every one of you, in the name of Jesus Christ for the forgiveness of and release from your sins; and you shall receive the gift of the Holy Spirit." (Also Acts 8:20).

Mercy

(Romans 9:15, 16).

God's gifts are to be used

Romans 12:6-8 (AMPC), "Having gifts (faculties, talents, qualities) that differ according to the grace given us, let us use them: [He whose gift is] prophecy, [let him prophesy] according to the proportion of his faith; 7 [He whose gift is] practical service, let him give himself to serving; he who teaches, to his teaching; 8 He who exhorts (encourages), to his exhortation; he who contributes, let him do it in simplicity and liberality; he who gives aid and superintends, with zeal and singleness of mind; he who does acts of mercy, with genuine cheerfulness and joyful eagerness."

A gift from God is never withdrawn

Romans 11:29 (AMPC) "For God's gifts and His call are irrevocable. [He never withdraws them when once they are given, and He does not change His mind about those to whom He gives His grace or to whom He sends His call.]"

The Holy Spirit is a gift from God

1 Corinthians 6:19 (AMPC) "Do you not know that your body is the temple (the very sanctuary) of the Holy Spirit Who lives within you, Whom you have received [as a Gift] from God? You are not your own."

Celibacy is a gift from God.

1 Corinthians 7:7 (AMPC) "I wish that all men were like I myself am [in this matter of self-control]. But each has his own special gift from God, one of this kind and one of another." (Also Matthew 19:10, 11).

All gifts come from God in Heaven.

John 3:27 (AMPC) "John answered, A man can receive nothing [he can claim nothing, he can take unto himself nothing] except as it has been granted to him from Heaven. [A man must be content to receive the gift which is given him from Heaven; there is no other source.]"

All believers in Christ are a gift to Him from God the Father.

John 17:24 (AMPC), "Father, I desire that they also whom You have entrusted to Me [as Your gift to Me] may be with Me where I am, so that they may see My glory, which You have given Me [Your love gift to Me]; for You loved Me before the foundation of the world."

God gives spiritual gifts to those in the body of Christ as He sees fit.

1 Corinthians 12:1 (AMPC) "NOW ABOUT the spiritual gifts (the special endowments of supernatural energy), brethren, I do not want you to be misinformed."

1 Corinthians 12:4-6 (AMPC) "Now there are distinctive varieties and distributions of endowments (gifts, extraordinary powers distinguishing certain Christians, due to the power of divine grace operating in their souls by the Holy Spirit) and they vary, but the [Holy] Spirit remains the same. 5 And there are distinctive varieties of service and ministration, but it is the same Lord [Who is served]. 6 And there are distinctive varieties of operation [of working to accomplish things], but it is the same God Who inspires and energizes them all in all."

Since a gift is tied to a function, we all are given gifts because we all have functions.

1 Corinthians 12:27 (AMPC) "Now you [collectively] are Christ's body and [individually] you are

members of it, each part severally and distinct [each with his own place and function]."

Each person in the body of Christ is a gift from God to that body. But, I have learned that when a person doesn't know their function or calling, they will waste time on trivial stuff like he said, she said, and even being a busybody in other people's affairs. But when you know and understand your calling and function in the body of Christ, you don't have time or energy to get into minor stuff, because you are about your Father's business.

Again, I hope this whets your appetite as you desire to know more about the Kingdom of God. It really is a vast subject, but this is what God has given me. I pray that each of you continually seeks the Lord Jesus Christ. Thank Him for dying and shedding His blood for your sins and the worlds. Continue to walk by faith and not by sight in His Kingdom. Remember the differences between where the Kingdom is and where religion is. Wherever the Kingdom is, there is power. Wherever religion is, there is no power, just words, and talk. Jesus didn't just talk about God healing people. He actually healed them. Jesus didn't just talk about what God can do, or that He is can feed the multitudes. He actually used His Father's power to feed them.

May God bless you and keep you!

ABOUT THE AUTHOR

Pierce A. Smith has been in ministry for over 40 years. He has served in many capacities: Senior Pastor, Associate minister, youth minister, men's ministry leader, youth choir director/musician, praise and worship leader/musician, teacher and band member to name a few. Pierce has a Bachelors in Electronic Engineering Technology from the University of Dayton, an MBA from Hood College and a Specialist degree in Theology from Zoe University. Pierce currently sits on the Board of Directors of the Southeastern Correctional Ministry in the Hampton Roads area of Virginia.

Before coming to Virginia Beach and Suffolk, he pastored New Life Baptist Church in Gaithersburg, MD for ten years. He has ministered at the Manna Baptist Church in Chesapeake, VA, Our Daily Bread Cafe in Virginia Beach, Women in Shared Ministry (WISM) Leadership Conference, Light of Life

Christian Center in Chesapeake, VA, First Mount Olive Baptist Church in Leesburg, VA, and Ebenezer Baptist Church in Alexandria, VA, to name a few.

Pierce retired from Schneider Electric/Square D Company after 32 years and is now in full-time ministry as Pastor of the Abundant Glory Christian Center located in Suffolk, VA. His interests are in helping others discover their God-given assignments in the body of Christ and to experience the power and reality of God regularly. He also loves reading, sports, and traveling.

He is married to the Rev. Thelma C. Smith, his beautiful bride of 45 years. Together they have three adult children and six grandchildren.

INDEX

A

afterlife, 42
angels, 3, 6, 39, 65
atmosphere, 38
authority, 11, 15–17, 36–38, 69

B

blessings, 8, 10, 58

C

centurion, 15–16
Christianity, 22, 32, 64
Christians, 17, 70, 74
church, 28, 31, 48, 51–52, 56–57, 60, 66
counsel, 40

D

demons, 17–18, 20, 24, 28, 31, 49, 65, 68
denomination, 14
destiny, 43, 53, 55, 58
disciples, 30, 41, 43, 45, 48–49
discipleship, 18, 42–44, 68
divine, 59–60
dominion, 4, 16–17, 36–37

E

enemies, 8, 14–15, 68
eternity, 21, 42
exhortation, 72

F

faith, 7, 10, 16, 22, 24–25, 29, 32, 36, 53, 56–57, 69, 72, 75
forgiveness, 54, 71

G

gifts, 48–49, 55–56, 59, 69, 71–75
glory, 25, 37, 49, 62, 74
Good News, 10, 27, 29, 31–32, 35–38

gospel, 10, 20, 27, 29–30, 35, 37–42, 46, 53–54, 65

government, 1–2, 4, 9–12, 14–20, 22–23, 25, 31, 35, 37–38, 51–52, 69–71

grace, 5–6, 10–11, 25, 29, 34–35, 47, 55–56, 71–72

H

hearts, 5, 20, 33, 54, 57, 60–61, 63, 66
Heaven's government, 20
Holy Spirit, 3–4, 34, 43, 50, 54, 65, 67–68, 71–74
honor, 12, 58

I

ideology, 10–11, 22
idol, 37
immortality, 35
institution, 11

J

justice, 4, 9, 15, 17, 70

K

kingdom, 1–2, 4, 6, 8–12, 17–24, 27–44, 46, 48–52, 54–55, 59, 63–71, 75 knowledge, 47

L

laws, 6–8, 10, 14–15, 25, 27–29, 34, 41, 45–46
legal side, 17–18, 22
Lord, 2–4, 6, 16, 20, 24, 28, 36, 38, 41, 46, 52, 54, 70, 74

M

manifestation, 69
marriage, 3, 11
masterpiece, 44, 59
mediator, 7
mercy, 5, 34, 72
military, 14, 16, 20
ministers, 30, 69, 71, 77
miracles, 28
momentary affliction, 25
multitudes, 20, 40, 69, 75
murder, 4, 14

N

nation, 5, 12, 14–15, 32, 43

O

obedience, 41
opposition, 50

P

peace, 4, 49–50, 70
power, 3, 15–17, 20, 28–29, 34–35, 41, 48–50, 52, 59, 62, 64, 67–69, 74–75, 78
pray, 5, 50, 75
prayer, 13, 19, 54
preaching, 39–40, 67
prophets, 3, 7, 10, 27, 32, 46, 48, 56

R

religion, 5, 10–11, 21–22, 29, 41, 53, 75
righteousness, 9, 15, 18–19, 28, 70

S

salvation, 17–18, 28–30, 32, 52, 56, 68, 71
Savior, 32, 34–35, 41, 54
shame, 48, 53
sickness, 39–40, 49, 53
silver, 49, 57
sins, 2–3, 6–7, 11, 17, 20, 22, 24–25, 30, 34, 45, 47, 54, 68, 71, 75
sows, 8–9

T

truth, 11, 15, 17, 36, 45–46, 63

V

vision, 12, 60, 62

W

war, 14–15, 18
warfare, 17–18
wisdom, 9, 47, 71

Z

zeal, 4, 70, 72

www.ingramcontent.com/pod-product-compliance
Lightning Source LLC
Chambersburg PA
CBHW052202110526
44591CB00012B/2040